ON HIS
Path

ANNETTE HARTLEY

WESTBOW
PRESS
A DIVISION OF THOMAS NELSON

WestBow Press books may be ordered through booksellers or by contacting:

WestBow Press
A Division of Thomas Nelson
1663 Liberty Drive
Bloomington, IN 47403
www.westbowpress.com
1-(866) 928-1240

Because of the dynamic nature of the Internet, any web addresses or links contained in
this book may have changed since publication and may no longer be valid. The views
expressed in this work are solely those of the author and do not necessarily reflect the
views of the publisher, and the publisher hereby disclaims any responsibility for them.

Any people depicted in stock imagery provided by Thinkstock are models,
and such images are being used for illustrative purposes only.

Certain stock imagery © Thinkstock.

ISBN: 978-1-4908-0066-0 (sc)
ISBN: 978-1-4908-0068-4 (hc)
ISBN: 978-1-4908-0067-7 (e)

Library of Congress Control Number: 2013912006

Printed in the United States of America.

WestBow Press rev. date: 08/21/2013

TABLE OF CONTENTS

INTRODUCTION

I am thankful that I can reflect on the fact that God showed me His path and led me to it when I was very young. His promises along that path have been meaningful to me through the years: "You have made known to me the path of life." "In all your ways, acknowledge Him and He will direct your paths." "Show me your ways O Lord, teach me your paths." (Acts 2:28, Proverbs 3:6, Psalm 25:4)

In recent years I have come to recognize the extraordinary pattern God has woven in my life. The beginning of the pattern took place in 1895, long before I was born, when God called to the ministry a young boy as he sat with his parents in the sanctuary of Independent Presbyterian Church of Savannah, Georgia. This young boy grew up to be the great evangelical preacher, Daniel Iverson, who led me to Christ in 1939 in Miami, Florida. As God wove the various threads of every hue throughout

Annette Hartley

my life, He kept me "on His path". He eventually led me to worship at that very same Independent Presbyterian Church in Savannah as a member of that particular church family.

One woman's journey through the years as she deals with the heartbreak of widowhood and finds her way through the changes in her life, hopefully will encourage those women who have experienced or will experience similar challenges.

Part I

FROM HEARTBREAK

May 1982-May 1986

CHAPTER 1

Moonlit Friday night... Key West shrimp, pink and tender... French bread dripping lemon butter... Family: pregnant Anne with Ed, and a few intimates ... gathered poolside at the round table ... reminiscing ... planning Saturday golf game . . . laughing . . . fragrant, fun-filled evening... good-byes at the door.

Teen-age Emily and her two friends settling into quiet chatter... off to bed and off to sleep...Jim and I bringing in dessert plates, sticky with traces of Key Lime pie ... loading the dishwasher ... climbing stairs to our nightly retreat.,.just in time for 11 o'clock news... Ted Koeppel's incisive questioning, laying open the Argentine-Falklands crisis... May 1, l982 ... Drowsiness overtaking me

Then those words:: "Can I bring you a midnight snack?"... "Too sleepy"... "Night...I love you Baby".... "Love you too"

The empty bed . . . The light still burning . . . What time is it? . . . Where is he? Maybe taking his evening swim a bit late . . .

Sleepily down the stairs . . . Lights on in the bathroom, pajamas neatly folded. Can of asparagus open, partially eaten, on the counter . . . Lights on out back.

May Day . . . May Day . . . 911 . . . Bottom of the pool . . . Oh God, how can I reach him? Oh God Oh God Oh God . . . Wake the girls . . . Pray . . . Sirens . . . Rescuers leaping over the wall . . . Exhaustive human effort . . . Agony

Family all back now . . . holding on . . . praying together . . . God, take control of us . . . . God, You have promised never to leave us or forsake us . . . God, You have promised never to give us more than we can bear . . . God, You are the Potter, we are the clay . . . How can we presume to question Your will? But Oh God, how do we deal with this awful, awesome devastation? . . . You give and You take away . . . All things work together for good for those who love You and are called according to Your purpose . . . Oh God, You have orchestrated this event! You brought him to the peak of his career, his productivity at its height. Now you have taken him back. No more stress now, no more pain in the football knee, no growing old and feeble and senile, no more business anxieties or disappointments. You give and You take away. He's with

You now. You wipe away every tear. He is at peace. Oh God, help me to have peace for this moment.

My beloved leader . . . How can I breathe? Oh God, You are not the author of chaos and confusion. You have not given us the spirit of fear, but of power and love and a sound mind. Oh God, give me a sound mind. Give me grace and dignity that I might walk before my children, confident that in Christ we do not grieve as those who have no hope . . . . All these promises I've been taught through the years . . . Show me that they work, Lord . . . Your peace, not as the world gives peace, but Your peace that passes understanding: Give me that . . . Oh God, You who are the same yesterday, today and tomorrow, help me find my way through the changes in my life.

As we sat huddled, broken, devastated, in the kitchen, they removed my husband's body from the pool area. Examiners from the coroner's office were there with the fire rescue squad and our Coral Gables neighborhood police. They came to the door, murmured sorrowful sounds and took him away.

My 16 year-old Emily; pregnant Anne with husband Ed; middle daughter Claudia and her Tom airbound from Dallas . . . Violent interruption to life . . . none of us would ever be the same again.

CHAPTER 2

After everyone had left, Emily sobbed "Mom, come sleep in my room . . . You can't possibly sleep in that bed any more"

Emily, being alone in that bed is no harder than sitting at the breakfast table without him will be . . . or working in the yard without him . . . or turning on the television and not have him there. This house is filled with him.

Then I'm going to sleep in there with you, Mama . . . You're not staying there alone! Oh, Mom what are we going to do?

I don't know yet, darling; we have to take one step at a time

But Mom, will you have to go to work? Will I be able to go to college? Or should I try to get a job or what?

Emily, I don't really know the status of Dad's business or what his insurance program is. You know, the women of my generation were happy to have our husbands take care of money matters and to let them make decisions regarding business and so on. But I know Dad had some reversals in the last few years and it's possible that I will go to work at least until you're through with college.

But Mom, what can you do? You haven't ever worked before . . . You've always been home.

That's not true, Ems; you came along so late in our lives, you don't realize I was in retailing, and then did secretarial work and substitute teaching before Anne was born . . . Don't worry, we're going to be fine . . . Maybe I'll even get a job at Coral Gables High and we can go to school together every day.

Mom, I don't want to stay in this house without Daddy . . . I couldn't stand it . . . It would be so depressing . . . just you and me at the dinner table . . . Mom we just can't do it. Let's move to a condo like Biltmore II. Some of my friends at school live there . . . and I'll never be able to open the refrigerator here without seeing Daddy standing there . . . O Mama, I love him so much.

I know, darling . . . He was a wonderful father to you and a rock to me . . . All my identity and security is wrapped up in him . . . Only God Himself can take us through this. And oh Emily, just think! He missed by only a month seeing his first grandchild! He was so looking forward to knowing Anne and Ed's baby. Poor Anne . . . She was completely hysterical tonight. I think it's going to be harder for her than any of us. I'm glad she has Ed. He is a godsend for all of us.

Yes, I love him too . . . Wasn't it neat tonight when he came into the kitchen and put his arms around us and said he would take care of all of Jim's girls now . . . Oh Mama, can you believe we'll get up tomorrow and walk around in the world without Daddy?

Honey, let's try to concentrate on the things for which we can be thankful . . . Think how much harder it would be if Dad had walked out on us. Think of your friends who've had to deal with rejection and indifference when their fathers have left home. We know Dad loved us more than anything and that his leaving us was involuntary, an act of God . . . and think of the warm and wonderful memories of your 16 years with him.

Mom, do you think Dad would have gone through the torture of giving up smoking two years ago if he'd thought he had so short a time to live?

Oh Emily, I don't think he'd trade that feeling of satisfaction and pride of conquest for anything. As hard as it was, he experienced great victory in a battle he'd fought for 20 years.

When will Claudia and Tom get in, Mom? Don't you know it was awful for Claudia to get the message when she's so far away?

Yes, it had to be horrible! Uncle Dale spoke to Tom of course and let him break the news to her. I don't know the exact hour they're getting in, but I know they left Dallas an hour ago, so they're enroute right now. I've missed Laudi so much in all of this . . . Hers and Tom's absence has left a huge gap during this time of shock and heartbreak in our family's grieving. I can't wait for them to get here.

Mom, I called Jeff's parents at 2 this morning and they called Jeff at Key Club Convention and he's on his way home, too.

Oh Emily, I didn't dream you had done that . . . What did his Mom say?

She was wonderful. I need him to be here Mom, and she said he would want to be here with me . . . He loved Dad, too, you know.

Yes I know they were devoted to each other. I'll be glad to have him here, too. Emily, I know neither of us can go to sleep, but it's almost daybreak. Let's just try to lie quietly and rest until time to get up. We have to face tomorrow with dignity and grace and courage. Let's ask God to make it possible.

Mom, do you remember the story about the boy who walked with God all his life, and when he went to heaven he looked back over his life and saw two sets of footprints all the way except for several places over jagged rocks and there was only one set of prints . . . and he asked God why He had deserted and left him alone over the hard places . . . and God answered "That's when I carried you, my son". Well, that's what He'll have to do for us now, Mom. He'll have to carry us for a long, long time until I can make it without my Daddy.

CHAPTER 3

But Emily is young . . . life will normalize for her after long painful adjustment . . . and Anne's and Claudia's lives are secure with strong, loving, caring husbands . . . But I? My security, my very identity were in him . . . Where am I and who am I and where am I going without him? After 33 years of marriage to this dynamic Type-A decision-maker, do I have the facility for independent living on anything but the most basic level? Friends always said I lived a "charmed" life, given away by loving, protective father to adoring, protective husband, I had been sheltered from the harsh realities of life . . . No reason to concern myself with business, no knowledge about taxes, insurance, investments . . . always depended on his good judgment in these areas while I concentrated on family and home enrichment. Even this week I spoke with his financial advisor and learned there was no need for us to worry about the future, college expenses, etc. Jim had taken good care of us in his planning; but there were so many decisions facing me: Emily's schooling; I'm a single parent now ... a single homeowner. But remember, I graduated from college with honors . . . I know I have a good mind . . . but all these years it's been dedicated, committed to him and his career and his home and his children . . . The success and prestige which came to him, and his happiness in our marriage, have given me joy and fulfillment. Yet now, even in these first hours I must turn my thoughts away from preoccupation with the past . . . Oh God, give me grace and dignity to face tomorrow and to live it.

For the next two days, the house was filled with caring friends and family . . . An outpouring of love from our tri-ethnic community. Over 1200 people attended the memorial service at our Granada Presbyterian Church. He was appreciated.

The day following the service, I rose with inexplicable resolve to go downtown to his office. I was discouraged in this by loved ones who said, "It's too early to think of that. It's not necessary to push yourself to anything so difficult."

But for me it was absolutely necessary. The day was painful beyond description. His hallowed ground . . . his partner, his secretary of 14 years . . . the tears that flowed . . . the pictures in his office that spoke so warmly of the family man . . . the personal files, one for each of the girls, filled with sweet memorabilia . . . the dated stub of his last cigarette, smoked two years before . . .

the Orange Bowl past president's pin, the University of Miami Trustee card, the note on his calendar for Saturday's golf lesson . . . Painful but somehow building, strengthening to me.

The next day I gathered his brother, Jerry, and Ed and Tom and began going through all of his clothing and personal effects at home. The favorite cashmere sport coat fit Ed . . . the golf clubs to Jerry . . . the beloved old leather chair to Tom . . . The Brooks Brothers wardrobe dispersed among them and several dear friends . . . Tears ongoing, yet pain building endurance moment by moment. I felt it in body and spirit. God was leading me through the suffering to a new level of maturity. The words from Romans 5 came to me: "Rejoice in our sufferings because we know that suffering produces perseverance; perseverance, character; and character, hope."

Somehow the verifying of that truth by experiencing it personally, gave me a surge of power, of the desire to gain more control. I picked up my Bible and read Hebrews 12:11 "No suffering seems pleasant at the time but painful. Later on, however, it produces a harvest of righteousness and peace for those who have been trained by it."

Oh, yes, moment by moment I was stepping with more confidence, more assurance. Where before, I had planned to look to Jerry and the sons-in-law for leadership and decisions, now I was gaining control of my senses. The next deliberate step was to have a poolside supper before the family left town to return to their homes . . . and so a week after losing my beloved husband to a heart attack in our pool, I insisted that our family and closest friends go for a swim . . . It was a cathartic experience, and by the end of the evening, that pool no longer was an ominous, sinister symbol, but once more a place for good times, for remembering the happy hours spent there through the years. We emerged as from a baptism, cleansed in spirit and recognizing a certain newness of life.

And so it went ... step by step: Meetings with lawyers, brokers, advisers; learning terminology of the business world; making decisions about the house: Yes, I'll keep it. Yes, I can manage ... new roof, termite treatment, new arrangements for yard and pool care ... Yes, I must buy a new car ... Family trips and reunions ... Decision-making is coming easier as time goes on.

I reflect now on the person I was before the turning point. I like that person and understand her and wouldn't change the circumstances which made her as she was ... and yet, I wouldn't want to be that person again ...

The message I read in my children's eyes has moved from love and sympathy, even pity, to love and respect for one who has survived and arrived. I am grateful for that nuance of change. It is liberating to know experientially that, with God's unfailing guidance, I can find my way through the changes in my life.

CHAPTER 4

Dark, handsome and deadly serious, he came to us straight from Gordon Conwell Seminary in Boston. A proper Bostonian he could have been. His sober countenance, reserved manner, his very intensity... belied his California background, the youth complete with surfboard, Valley Girls and the Beta fraternity house.

His calling to the ministry had come while a long-haired senior at Southern Cal, in the mid-70s. Straightway he had determined to study under the famed theologian, Dr. James I. Packer, of Trinity College in Bristol, England. Of modest circumstances, he had worked, made loans from family and friends, obligated his future, in order to achieve this goal. Direct from the warmth of California's easy, mellow lifestyle, he thrust himself into the cold, harsh, metallic existence of Trinity College. Separation from family and friends, the icy showers, cold beds, and cool fellow students, caused him to seek God's face in a new and personal way . . . and Dr. Packer's academically challenging lectures honed his intellect, as they confirmed his calling, and strengthened his faith in the God he was to serve.

The time of internship in Scotland, rugged land of the great Reformers, living on meager rations in the homes of various parishioners whose cupboards were relatively bare, but whose hearts were warm and generous, gave him an added dimension which set him apart from the other young men who had served on our church staff. An austerity, a sparseness of words, an apparent disdain for light conversation caused consternation in many who met the new young intern . . . On the other hand, a passion for teaching and preaching the Word of God, an extraordinary capability of empathizing with those in pain, the obvious intensity of purpose to make a difference in the world . . . these qualities endeared him to the hearts of most of the congregation.

He came to live in our guest suite. He came to bring security and some measure of comfort and company to Emily and me now that we were alone. He had completed a year of internship and was contemplating a return to the northeast to earn an advanced degree, when the call came from our minister. There was a temporary need at the Billings home during this adjustment period. Could he stay awhile? The answer was immediate. He had spent time at that home during the weeks of the tragedy and felt a great soul-searing compassion for those two left alone . . . . the widow and the 16 year-old daughter. Yes, he was available.

With duffle bag and dirty clothes and stacks of old dusty books, Terry Johnson moved into our home one Saturday morning. Tall, slim and tanned, he wore wrinkled navy shorts and a "Southern Cal Trojan" tee-shirt.

Unsmiling, quiet and sensitive, he set about to bring a measure of spiritual help and support to us as we dealt with the awesome void in our lives. He sat with us whenever possible and observed; his conversation never idle words, always on point, always cutting through the superficial, laying open the real meaning of the exchange. He was able to recognize the slightest variation in mood: "You're having a hard time this morning, aren't you, Mrs. Billings? Do you want to talk about it?" Long monologues would ensue when I poured out what was heavy on my heart, reaching back far into the past as I answered his questions about my husband. He never seemed to tire of hearing the smallest details of personality or situation . . . and the more I spoke, the more the gloom lifted. Over time, this young man was allowing me a complete catharsis.

As I knew him more intimately, I was surprised to find in him a vulnerability and needfulness that was not apparent upon superficial acquaintance. He was 27. All his adult years had been spent in the ivory tower of academia, and in fervent and passionate pursuit of God's truth. There was a crying need for warmth and intimate companionship and tender caring, for the love of a woman. It was at this point that I decided God had put him in our lives for a purpose . . . I set out to find him a wife.

CHAPTER 5

At the beginning, this experiment in a type of communal living, proved mutually beneficial, as Terry, the Youth Minister, became our intimate friend and comforter during the dreaded loneliness, and our home provided family warmth for him.

He had walked into our home and immediately become my confidante, quiet, reserved, yet concerned about Emily's and my well-being, and eager to be of assistance. On occasion I would go to him to discuss a decision to be made regarding Emily's lifestyle at the big public high school. His spiritual maturity and training in counseling gave validity to his views and I valued his input.

At the same time, Emily respected him and, as most of her peers in the church Youth Group, looked at him, with certain stars in her eyes. Terry, the brilliant, the handsome, the cool, who could have been a worldly success in any field, had chosen to give and live his life serving God.

This was a combination which evoked sighs and warm emotion from females sixteen to sixty.

After the first month, however, the intimacy of living under one roof, led to moments of disenchantment, for as Terry became more involved in our lives and confidence developed between us, he began to assert himself in areas in which he found Emily's conduct to be wanting. At 16, she was mature beyond her years in dealing with serious situations and in people skills, but every bit the teenage prototype in tight jeans, short shorts, emotional outbursts, heavy high school romance, spasmodic lapses in study preparation, occasional rebellious words to parent, and an aversion to housework.

One Saturday morning in our kitchen during a confrontation with her mother, Terry interjected: "Emily, you should not to speak to your mother in that disrespectful way." With body language speaking furiously, she turned on him: "Terry Johnson, you can stay in this house but you had better not start meddling in our affairs, do you hear? My mother and I have gotten along just great for 16 years and we don't need you to mediate!" and she stormed out.

Other times were less violent, even lighthearted, but nonetheless the relationship of the Youth Group teenage girl with crush on Youth Minister gradually evolved to something akin to big brother/little sister, in which there was complete liberty to disagree, argue, battle and sulk, before reconciliation occurred.

After a particularly unpleasant incident between them, Terry came to me with the complaint that Emily was being most unreasonable and he thought I should intervene . . . My response was that she wasn't being unreasonable with me and that all her other relationships seemed to be going well . . . so it was up to him to work it out with her, just as he probably would have to do with difficult members of his church congregation in the future.

He set a time to talk it out with her and asked me to sit in on the discussion. At each point, Emily held her own in the argument, giving valid reasons for her position and accusing him of being arbitrary. As I sat busily doing my needlepoint, I wondered at her poise and ability to articulate in the heat of battle with so powerful an adversary. She was not overmatched. The stand-off was a challenge for Terry, and although no victory was won, he felt satisfied that the airing was cleansing and restoration of good will had taken place. Not so with Emily. She walked away from the confrontation with cold and distant eyes and turned from the proffered hand and paternal hug.

Three days later, Terry anxiously asked: "How can I get Emily back to normal again? She won't have a thing to do with me." I answered that I certainly couldn't legislate in the matter and it was entirely up to him to deal with that problem.

The next morning I walked into the living room to find Terry and Emily in warm embrace, Emily crying, Terry wiping away her tears. Restoration had taken place.

After that moment there was no obvious change, yet everything was different. I continued in the role to which I felt God had called me. I arranged meetings and dates for the young minister with a number of beautiful committed Christian women, some of them flight attendants who attended the Singles Bible Studies at Key Biscayne Presbyterian Church ... I even had him go up to Orlando to meet an especial favorite of mine.

At Christmastime, my family, including my brother-in-law and his wife and three children, along with my dearest friend and her family, all joined me in going away for the holidays. It was just too painful to stay at home this first Christmas, hearing all the familiar carols, spending this special family time without my beloved husband. We rented a lodge in Highlands, North Carolina and had an old-fashioned country Christmas there, all missing him together. We had sweet times every evening with the men taking turns in leading our devotions as we quietly, worshipfully celebrated our Savior's birth.

On Christmas Eve, I received a phone call from Terry, who, of course, had remained at home. I had left him my Dolphin football tickets, and arranged for him to take a lovely girl to dinner and to the game. Here was the gist of the conversation: Mrs. Billings, I've decided I want you to stop arranging dates for me . . . I'm tired spending my time and money on strangers. I've decided I want to wait for Emily . . . "You can't be serious", I gasped. She's 16 years old . . . . She has a year and a half left of high school and four years of college . . . . :You can't wait that long . . . You're too needful right now!" From that moment on, a type of low key battle ensued between the two of us. Devoted deeply to each other and desiring the best for my daughter, we gently proceeded to attack and counter-attack, our positions shifting, winning some, losing some.

The shocking news that the serious, committed young minister was in love at 27 with a teen-ager complete with braces and little-boy fingernails, was beyond my comprehension. We agreed that he should move from our home immediately. The whole picture had changed . . . He no longer was a role model in the absence of her father, nor my confidante to help in advising her during these high school years . . . . So, one more debilitating change shook my day to day existence.

Chapter 6

Here I suffered another type of loss . . . another emotional stronghold had been removed from my life . . . I had learned to depend on this person on a daily basis and his presence was strengthening to me as I found my way, living as single homeowner, parent, and widow . . . Terry had become a part of my decision-making process, of my approach to running of the household . . . . Immediately I insisted that he meet with Dr. Baird (our senior pastor) and tell him of his attachment to one of the youth of the church . . . I was sure Jim Baird would have him move on, as it would be awkward when word got out that the Youth Minister was romantically drawn to one of the young girls . . . .

On the contrary, Dr. Baird received the news with the admonition: That's fine, Terry, if you're sure you can handle strong-blooded women because those Billings women are that! He then proceeded to lay out stringent guidelines for the relationship: He was not to be alone with Emily until she came home for Thanksgiving during her first year at college. (Now, remember, she was in her junior year of high school!) Emily was not made aware of the situation at this time, and continued with activities at her school as well as her romance with Jeff, her high school boyfriend.

Somehow I felt it necessary to have my trusted lifelong friends, Alice Gene and Dale Anderson, to share in this with me . . . Dale was an elder in our church, and of course they were well acquainted with Terry. With his permission, I had them come to dinner and he confided in them his intentions . . . It was comforting to me to have them understand and just to be there for me during this unusual and somewhat stressful time.

In her senior year, Emily was chosen to be the Chaplain at her high school, and when she found out that she would not be allowed to read from the Bible, she was horrified . . . She came home upset and furious and called Terry for advice. This brought them together to talk over the details of how to react, and what could be done . . . The principal stated that it was a rule which came from the School Board, and the school had no alternative but to obey it. Terry called a committee of the Youth Group to meet with them over a period of time to plan strategy . . . The outcome was that Emily called the School Board office, requesting an opportunity for her, as well as a committee from her Youth Group, to appear before the Board to plead their case. The permission was granted and they were to be at the next meeting . . . Three days before the meeting, the lawyer for the School Board called her at home and told her that the rule had been misstated, and of course she would be allowed to read the Bible, along with other accepted religious works. The church Youth Group felt God had truly intervened in this case, and this represented a shared victory, particularly for the Chaplain and the Youth Minister.

Very gradually Emily began to notice the change in Terry's dealings with her, and seemed to be honored that our Youth Minister had chosen her to be special in his life, when there were many lovely girls the ages of her older sisters, who would have been pleased at his attentions.

The summer following graduation, Terry very much wanted to take Emily to Scotland to meet his dear friends and the pastors who had ministered to him during his internship there. His experience among these people had impacted his life enormously, and he deeply desired that they meet the young woman he had chosen to share his life . . . even more, he wanted her to know them. Consequently, Emily, Terry and I had a lovely 10-day trip to the Land of the Great Reformers.

I rented the car, and he drove us through the gorgeous countryside, always knowing the exact charming inn in which to stop and have tea and shortbread, as well as the perfect place to lunch for fish'n chips . . . In Aberdeen, we met the famed Scottish theologian, Mr. William Still, under whose influence Terry had garnered such amazing insights, particularly in the field of prayer. We were hosted in the home of a family who had been very meaningful to him . . . He was the caretaker at the church as well as at a nearby school, and these cherished friends insisted upon giving up their bed to Emily and me, while they slept on the sofas . . . We experienced the warmest Scottish hospitality, and left after two nights, feeling deeply connected to these dear people.

We traveled to beautiful St. Andrews; in Edinburgh, we were able to attend the thrilling Tattoo in the outdoor stadium. This annual event corresponds to our 4th of July. The program closed with the Bagpiper on the cliff above, playing "Amazing Grace". Our trip to Scotland was a wonderful and sentimental journey, and I was grateful for the opportunity to play chaperone!

In the fall, Emily left for Vanderbilt University . . . It was decided that she should be open to dating and making the most of her freshman year at college. Terry encouraged her in this, and of course I felt it was important as well. They stayed in touch, however, and when he knew she had a date, he very sweetly sent her yellow roses. True to the plan Dr. Baird outlined a year and a half before, when Emily came home for Thanksgiving, they appeared together and began publicly dating. Still no one dreamed it was anything more than friendship which was natural since he had lived at our house during the time after her father's death.

At the end of that freshman year, I felt very strongly that since their affection for each other had continued to grow, Emily should stay home and attend the University of Miami, so that they could truly spend time together . . . She had been a social butterfly, and I wanted her to know how different her life would be if she were married to a minister, whose Saturday nights most probably would be spent in prayer and preparation for the Lord's Day.

This plan was adopted, she living in the dorm, and they seeing each other as much as possible. All seemed to be going well until one night after they had picnicked on the beach, they came home early, and she ran up the stairs crying. I

33

knocked on the door of her room to see if she needed me, and she said "Oh, Mom, Terry told me tonight that if we got married, I could never spend another Christmas at home . . . He said we would always have to be with our church family!" That was a heartbreaking thought to one who always had been part of a close-knit, holiday-loving, inter-generational family. Although she was obviously upset, we talked through the subject, discussing the fact that in every dramatic change in one's life, there would be circumstances that might not be to our liking. Would this be something that would be important enough for her to want to re-consider her plans? All I could think of for the moment was how wise Terry had been to break such news at this point, rather than after they married when it would be a devastating shock to the young bride.

Although I had felt strongly that no marriage should occur until after my daughter had earned her college degree, I must admit to being very much in sympathy with them when they so desired to begin their life together at the end of her second year of college . . . Terry had waited for her for four years; he was now 31, so the date was set for May 23, 1986, just weeks after her 20th birthday.

They were to be married, of course, at our home church, Granada Presbyterian, and, as had been the custom in our family, the reception was to be held at the Riviera Country Club of Coral Gables. This had been the scene of mine as well as of her two sisters' receptions . . . Plans were well under way, when the acting pastor of our church (Dr. Baird had accepted a call to First Presbyterian Church of Jackson, Miss.) Rev. Danny Levi, called and invited me to come to his home for an important visit. Danny was young and although very dear to all of our family, I believe it took great courage for him to stop me in my tracks with the strong admonition that we just could not have a private country club reception . . . The church was Terry's family, since he had been on staff for almost five years, and all should be included . . . I have to admit to shedding some tears in the Levis' living room, but of course immediately understood and agreed with his premise. I have been grateful for his honesty and strength of conviction ever since.

With that decided change of venue, all family and friends and the whole church body, joined in preparations for this special event . . . Three ministers participated in the ceremony, including the Rev. Peter White who had been one of Terry's mentors from Scotland, as Emily's Uncle Jerry gave her away in lieu of his brother, her late father . . . The reception was held on the lovely church grounds, covered by large white canopies, chandeliers hanging from the ceiling, and palm and ficus trees banked all around . . . Violinists played from the church steps, and supper was served by Laura Ashley-clad young waitresses to more than 900 guests. A memorable evening indeed.

As my youngest daughter and her husband were driven to the airport to leave for their honeymoon, by Uncle Jerry and Aunt Patsy, I stood bereft, hardly able to imagine my life now without these two who had so filled it for the four years since Jimmy's death. However, at this moment I was struck with the thought that this wonderful event which had just taken place never would have happened except for the tragic circumstances which had brought Terry Johnson to live in our home. This unlikely romance between the serious and mature Youth Minister and the free-spirited teen-age girl in the Youth Group developed as God once more took the dark threads of sadness and wove them into the beautiful tapestry for our good and His glory.

And so in His divine wisdom, He led us on His chosen path; not the path we would have selected, through the heartbreak of losing husband and father. Yet we are told: "He restores my soul. He guides me in the paths of righteousness for His name's sake." (Psalm 23:3)

Part II

FINDING MY WAY
May 1982-November 2006

CHAPTER 1

For those weeks following Jim's sudden death, our goal for each day was to survive and learn to live in this world without our beloved husband and father.

The shock of it had been almost unbearable for daughter Anne, who was eight months pregnant with our first grandchild. Being the oldest daughter, and being very much the business woman, she and her father had a close and totally devoted relationship. (At one time, before they were able to lick the habit, they enjoyed their coffee and cigarettes together).

One month and eight days after his death, Anne went into labor. It was a bittersweet time, as Jim had so anticipated this event, and as happy as all of us were to have the time upon us, still there was sadness as we gathered at South Miami Hospital to await the birth. We were blessed to have a large group of special friends and ministers to sit and wait with us while Anne and Ed were laboring. Later, her doctor told us that was the largest non-Latin group he had ever seen sit out the labor in the hospital waiting room.!

Margaret Annette McDougall was born June 9th on her great grandmother Billings' birthday, just a little over a month after her grandfather's death. A tradition in our family had been that the name "Anne" alternated each generation with the name "Annette" . . . This had been true for at least seven generations . . . This time the name was given, but we couldn't resist the temptation to call this bright-eyed, lively baby girl "Maggie McDougall."

Maggie brought great joy to all of us, but I must admit that every time I took to the rocking chair with her, I wept to realize her adoring grandfather would never be able to hold and love her.

One of the difficult adjustments to widowhood at such a relatively young age was finding myself a single among the numerous gatherings of couples, both at church and in the community. Very soon I was led to start opening the doors of our home on a regular basis for fellowship times for the many singles in our church. Located within walking distance, our home became a place of retreat for the young unmarried. I took great pleasure in having these young adults for special occasions, holidays, and then just for conversation and socializing.

In January of 1985, our family was wonderfully blessed by the birth of James Billings McDougall. How we welcomed that new baby boy, particularly in light of the fact that Jim and I had never had a son, but three daughters instead.

In spite of the wonderful blessing of having my grandson join our family, 1985 brought new challenges to my quality of life for, as a widow, I had come to rely greatly upon Anne and Ed as my nearest and dearest support team. That year, however, Ed had a business opportunity which caused them to move to Orlando, five hours away from us, and it was very difficult to have them leave the little house in Coral Gables that they had occupied just walking distance from our home.

Thankfully, besides our church family and caring friends, among my closest and most important caregivers were Jerry and Pat Billings . . . Jerry was Jim's younger brother, and although they had moved from Miami to Orlando, where Jerry practiced law, they literally were at my side whenever there was a need . . . I visited them from time to time and they were with me often.

Soon after Anne and Ed's move, I went to Orlando to help Pat and Jerry get ready for a very special trip to China... The Republic of China had opened the Chinese Pavilion at Epcot in Disney World... The Chinese Pavilion was a place of world renown as soon as it opened because of the magnificence of its presence . . . In honor of the occasion, the Republic of China had invited dignitaries from Orlando, including Mayor Bill Fredericks and a number of state business leaders and their wives, as guests of the Chinese government, to tour their country... It was exciting to be involved, and I was experiencing a vicarious thrill just helping them plan their packing and travel.

I returned home on Sunday and on Monday night I received a phone call from the Mayor's attaché saying the Mayor's wife had broken her leg in a skiing accident and there were only 15 people now able to go, and would I possibly be able to get ready in time to join them so the 16th place would not be wasted! Of course I could never pass up such an opportunity, so for the next 24 hours, I stayed on the phone with officials arranging an emergency visa for me, went to the airport at 6 AM to get all my information and passport on the early plane which was met in Washington by an official who got it all in the works in record time so that I could meet the crowd in San

Francisco and leave the country on Thursday morning . . .
We flew out on May 18th . . . Pat and I roomed together
and Jerry roomed with the Mayor in his wife's absence.

Truly it was the experience of a lifetime, being wined
and dined and receiving the red carpet treatment from
the Chinese government . . . We arrived in Beijing . . .
There we saw the Ming Tombs, the Great Wall, the
Summer Palace, Tiananmen Square and the Imperial
Palace; we visited the Buddhist pagoda at the crest of the
palace grounds . . . There were state dinners every night;
we were honored with gourmet roast duck, jellyfish, sea
slugs, white fungus soup, birds'nest soup, camel tendon
soup, and greenish gelatinous "thousand-year-old" eggs
among other rare delicacies . . . We smiled and struggled
with our chopsticks. We were taken to five other Chinese
cities, including Shanghai, Suzhou and Guilin . . . we went
to Xian to see the famed terra cotta soldiers . . . We ended
our VIP visit to the Republic of China, and closed out our
incredibly wonderful tour in Hong Kong, from where we
took our Pan American Airways flight back to Orlando,
arriving on June 2nd.

I reflected later upon the fact that dear Joanne
Fredericks, the Mayor's wife, was forced to miss this
memorable two-week event because of her unfortunate

accident on the slopes . . . I realized that she was a beautiful Christian, worshiping the same great and loving God that I did . . . for some reason, this sad turn of events for her had become an incredibly wonderful gift for me! It affected my thinking for all the future happenings in my life: that sometimes a near-tragedy, even heartbreak, for a person or a family, possibly could be used in a positive and mighty way in the lives of others.

CHAPTER 2

Five years had passed now since Jim's sudden and shocking death . . . . During the first months, I fought constantly to stave off loneliness and depression, particularly at certain times of the day or week . . . A number of times I came home late in the afternoon, went into the empty house, and turned immediately, drove to the golf course, and played nine holes of golf all by myself . . . Being outdoors, walking on the beautiful golf course helped me through that lonesome hour of the day . . . Sometimes I went straight home afterward, others I would stop by for a visit with dear friends who lived nearby . . . At any rate, it was easier to go home alone after that relaxing and enjoyable activity . . .

After a time, my life assumed a type of normalcy which actually surprised me. I of course had continued with my usual activities . . . deep involvement at my church, teaching Bible in Circle, opening my home which was near the church, to various retreats and events, particularly for the young singles with whom I felt a real connection. Becoming single again at this time of my life, brought a new awareness to me of the sense of loneliness, and of separation, often felt by singles, although surrounded by caring friends, a support group, and various especially planned activities at the church. So much of the teaching centers on couples, the family, and child raising, as it certainly should, but often those who are alone have the feeling of being insignificant, out of the mainstream. We made a point of gathering the singles together to celebrate holidays, and let them know they were welcome to drop in and to have socials at our home throughout the year.

Besides my involvement at church, I was spending time with friends, playing in several bridge groups . . . and was included in dinner parties, University of Miami events, and Orange Bowl affairs. Since Jim had been vice chairman of the UM Board of Trustees, the University President was thoughtful to invite me along with the dignitaries who traveled with the Hurricane football team to the various away games . . . One year I flew with them to New Orleans to the Sugar Bowl . . . Another I went to Tempe, Arizona to the Fiesta Bowl.

A subconscious fear which had assailed me since the first weeks after Jimmy's death was that the sons-in-law, Ed McDougall and Tom Waters, who had connected so absolutely with him, were now going to have little desire to spend vacation time with the widow .... Both were in real estate-related careers and Jim's being in real estate development, gave them a bond and a basis for animated discussion for hours.

Because of this subliminal concern which, I must admit, hounded my thoughts, I began to ponder ideas as to how I could deal with it. Jim had left money in trust for the girls and me, over and above the insurance which covered our living expenses . . . I called a long distance conference with Anne in Orlando, Claudia in Austin, and Emily in Savannah, and got their enthusiastic approval of my plan . . . I would spend that summer in North Carolina, which was our usual summer retreat from the heat of Miami, and begin to look for a piece of property on which we could build a vacation home.

My first thought was Highlands, as we had spent many summers there, and felt particularly connected because so many Miami people had vacation homes in that area . . . Besides that, it was particularly charming . . . .

It was not easy for me to make the decision to lay out that kind of capital; I never had felt comfortable spending great sums of money on my own; the biggest purchase I ever had made was my car . . . Even then I had asked a friend and elder in my church to accompany me as I shopped from dealer to dealer, for I had been told that lone women car buyers were easy prey to salesmen who could recognize naivete and lack of knowledge and experience. At any rate, I purchased a beautiful lot on the Highlands Country Club property, and began to investigate possible builders, etc.

My priority for the next month was to go to Memphis, Tennessee to attend my beloved maiden aunt who was to have eye surgery . . . She was like a second mother to me, and of course had no children of her own . . . She had taught school for 40 years, and after retirement, had been involved totally in caring for her mother, my grandmother, who had lived to be 105! After her death in 1985, I had hoped to get my aunt ("Sister") to come live with me and let me give her the kind of loving care she had given my grandmother . . . We tried this for a time, but she simply was not happy living so far from her roots, so returned to her apartment in Memphis and was comfortable living there alone.

Before I had an opportunity to return to Highlands, I was invited to spend a couple of weeks with friends in a North Carolina golf community called "Hound Ears" . . . (The name was taken from the huge rocks at the top of the mountain, which were amazingly shaped like a hound's two large ears) . . . It was across the state from Highlands, nestled in the Blue Ridge Mountains between Boone and Blowing Rock . . . It was gated, had tennis courts and a beautiful golf course behind the gate, as well as a gorgeous natural rock swimming pool . . . There were fine dining facilities, including a formal dining room, as well as snack shop available at lunchtime for golfers and hikers, etc. I found very attentive service people who were on call 24/7 if there were a need. Thinking of all that lay before me in the process of building a house, I began to consider the feasibility of perhaps finding a house on the market in this lovely place. I planned to go home and consult with the girls about this possible change in plans.

Before leaving for home from this beautiful "Hound Ears", I received a call from daughter Anne in Orlando, suggesting that I come by their home to celebrate my September 28th birthday . . . To be honest, I had been having a bit of a "pity party" thinking of my 60th birthday without benefit of loving, caring partner to gift me with the romantic flowers, jewelry and/or perfume . . . Jimmy and I always had made a special time of particular landmark birthdays and this big 6-O certainly fit in that category. . . . I was delighted that Anne and Ed had thought to do this and I accepted with great pleasure . . .

I drove to their home on September 27th and had a lovely supper and evening with them . . . The next morning (my actual 60th birthday,) I rose to the aroma of Anne's wonderful bran muffins, walked into the kitchen only to be met by Claudia and Tom (now living in Fort Myers, Florida) and Emily and Terry from Savannah! All the girls and their dear husbands had realized the importance of this occasion for me . . . . and had sacrificed in order to come together to celebrate with me . . . . They had arranged a lovely luncheon at a charming restaurant on Park Avenue in Winter Park . . . . and completed the picture with flowers, plus gifts of my favorite perfume and topping it off with an elegant sapphire lavalier (my birthstone) encrusted with diamond chips! Never have the love and thoughtfulness of anyone so moved and gratified my heart. Leaving my precious daughters and their husbands after the mountaintop experience there together, I praised God for His grace in bringing about such a totally unexpected and beautiful family expression of love and caring

In December of 1987 I signed the contract at Hound Ears to purchase a charming rustic cottage, hanging above hole #six of the golf course . . . it was only two bedrooms and two baths, so I located a highly respected builder in the area and added a bottom floor, which already had been plumbed and prepared for expansion . . . The additional space provided two more bathrooms, two bedrooms, a bunk room, sitting room and small half-kitchen . . . This would allow the three daughters and their husbands to have their own private bedrooms, with plenty of space for their children on the bunks, sofas, air mattresses, etc. Both floors opened onto decks overlooking the golf course with a breathtaking view of the mountains . . .

I believe with all my heart that God arranged the circumstances which gave me the opportunity to visit Hound Ears before I proceeded with my plans to build in Highlands . . . I sold my lot there with no difficulty, and work was begun on the addition in January 1988.

CHAPTER 3

In January of '88, in Miami, I attended the wedding of the daughter of dear friends . . . At the reception I met and visited with Bill and Tina Lane . . . Bill had been a fraternity brother and good business buddy of Jim's . . . . At the time of Jim's death, Bill had taken over our kitchen and organized all the meals that were brought in for the week . . . He had been a special help to me during that time, but I had seen him very little during the ensuing years. That night he, with his characteristic needle, remarked: "Well, I'm glad you haven't let yourself go completely to pot in the last few years." . . .

He followed that with the suggestion that he had a buddy who had roomed with him at Duke, who had lost his wife two years before and wondered if I would be interested in meeting him sometime . . . I casually answered in the affirmative although I didn't expect to hear any more from him on the subject . . . and that would be fine with me as I had no desire for another man n my life . . . I had been to dinner and to special occasions from time to time, with gentleman friends, but never with any feeling of wanting to see them more or to form any kind of relationship . . . Billy proceeded to tell me this man had been a scholar-athlete at Duke and afterward had played for the Pittsburgh Steelers . . . I, being a real football fan, was impressed with the credentials, but actually gave no more thought to the subject.

Two weeks later I received a call that this gentleman, Howard Hartley of Greenville, South Carolina, would be coming down to Miami to attend the Red Cross Ball with the Lanes and would I like to be his date? I went to the dance; he was by far the best dancer I had ever known . . . we danced all the way through dinner, hardly getting to the filet mignon before the dessert course . . . We had a delightful evening, and at the door when I thanked him and offered him my cheek, he took my face in his hands and kissed me lightly on the lips . . . Needless to say, I definitely had the desire to see more of this gentleman . . . he fell into an entirely different category from anyone I had seen since becoming a widow.

He asked me to go to brunch at the Biltmore Hotel with him and a group of the Lanes' friends, and I regretted, saying that I would love to, but would be going to church, as this would be Sunday morning . . . He said he'd pick me up after church . . . We then went to the Lanes' to watch a Duke basketball game, after which he asked me to dinner . . . I replied "sorry, I'm going to church", and he promptly said "we'll go after church" . . . Our hours together were easy and fun as we spoke of our respective families as well as the loss of our mates and how we had dealt with those . . . Howard came down to see me several times, and one night suggested that I might come to Greenville to meet his friends . . .

At this point, I realized that I had to be open and honest with him, as there was one deep concern in my heart which I had not made known . . . My words were something like this: One thing you need to know about me and it may turn you off completely, but I am a serious, hard-core Christian . . . God has met my needs, especially since Jim's death, in a supernatural way . . . I have felt His presence every hour and He has kept me from loneliness and despair. He has been so faithful to keep all the promises He gave us in Scripture . . . I simply can't take one step back from Him for any reason . . . I realize you don't share this type of faith as you have never offered to go to church with me or even mentioned any spiritual aspect of your life . . . So, as much as I have enjoyed getting to know you, I honestly believe we had better break this off.

Howard replied that he wished he could share this faith, but he just didn't see things that way . . . He told me he had been a steward in his church for 20 years, but that he never had studied the Bible or taken it too seriously.

We said good-bye and he returned to Greenville . . . At that time, I began to pray thus: Lord, You surely have given me this warm and loving feeling about this man, but I know You do not want me to continue in a relationship that would not honor You . . . So here <u>ver batim</u> is what I prayed almost daily: "Lord, if this man is supposed to be an important part of my life, please send someone to Greenville, South Carolina to impact his life for Christ." I did not mention to Howard anything about this prayer, nor did I ever refer to my faith again in our phone conversations.

I remember particularly that those wonderful words from Psalm 37 kept coming to me: "Delight yourself in the Lord and He will give you the desires of your heart." . . . . but I felt strongly that I couldn't trust the desires of my heart . . . So I prayed rather: I delight myself in You, but I want You to give me the desires of <u>Your</u> heart for me.

About six weeks later, I received a call from Howard at 11 o'clock one night and he related to me the following: "You'll never guess what happened tonight! I attended a dinner party with a lady who invited me as her escort, and it turned out to be an Executive Ministries outreach dinner . . . The speaker was a man who had been a World War II ace (Howard's war, in the Navy), was governor of South Dakota, and was president of the American Football League . . . He reminded me of Will Rogers as he kept us laughing the whole time until near the end, he gave his Christian testimony and it brought tears to my eyes . . . They passed around a sheet asking anyone who was interested in a weekly Bible study to sign up . . . Well I signed up and will start going next Wednesday morning at 6:00."

God had sent the Honorable Joe Foss to Greenville, South Carolina to impact Howard's life for Christ!

You can imagine the overwhelming effect this had on me! My hand trembled as I hung up the telephone, and from that moment on, felt that God was making possible my continuing relationship with this special man. Just imagine! God sent a man who was in Howard's age bracket, had fought in his war, and was president of a professional football league when Howard had played pro ball for the Steelers! What a good and gracious God we have.

I might add that Howard did indeed attend that Wednesday morning, and for the rest of his life, never missed a week unless we were out of town. It was a big part of his life, and of his exciting growth in the Lord.

At this point, my three daughters became like three caring mothers, hovering over this new situation . . . Claudia and Tom, living in Ft. Myers, had us over for a weekend so they could get to know this new person in mother's life . . . They prepared an elaborate beach picnic supper, complete with champagne and Tom's perfectly grilled steaks over the fire...A gorgeous sunset completed our evening at beautiful Sanibel Island...When Claudia asked Howard how he liked their extraordinary island, I could have wrung his neck when he answered: "I've had a great time and everything was wonderful, but if you call this rocky sand a beach, wait until you come to Litchfield Beach in South Carolina!"

(Here I have to inject that although we had never heard of Litchfield Beach, the first time Tom and Claudia visited us there, they fell in love with the untouched beauty and the powdery sand, and promptly bought a beach condo beside ours)

We visited Anne and Ed and their two children Maggie (six) and Jimmy (three) in Orlando, as well as Emily and Terry in Savannah . . . Emily was pregnant with their first... Naturally it was a bit difficult for them to imagine their mother with a man taking their father's place . . . Maggie and Jimmy and Howard had a warm and happy relationship from the start, as Howard was a true child-lover and they could tell it.

The next step was for me to go to Greenville, and get to know his two adult children, Paul in his early thirties and Cathy 29...Neither was married although both were in serious relationships . . . I have no doubt that they had the same reservations about someone moving into their father's life that my girls had experienced.

When I first visited Greenville, I stayed with friends of the family, and was delighted to know these warm and charming people . . . Another happy surprise to me was that Howard drove a late model grey Buick Park Avenue . . . Why was that important? I really don't know, except that it was conservative and handsome and somehow I was relieved, for I had only seen him in Miami in my environment.

Then, when he took me to see his townhouse, I was even more gratified, for his home was filled with antiques, lovely appointments and wall hangings. When he showed me the beautiful old quilts, handmade by his mother, I exclaimed how perfect they would be for my mountain house, and since he had them stored on the closet shelves, not in use, he should let me borrow them . . . His answer was: "No, they're part of my dowry; you may get to use them some day."

Cathy was living and working in Greenville and she and Howard enjoyed a loving and intimate father/daughter relationship . . . Paul had a fine career in real estate in Columbia, but came for the few days I was there so we could get acquainted . . . Altogether I would have to say we got off to a good start; if there were doubts or fears, they were not made known . . .

However, I felt sure it would be difficult for Cathy, since, as an only daughter, she had been so involved, since her mother's death three years before, in caring for her dad . . .

not that he wasn't out and about, dating and socializing with his many longtime friends, but she had maintained daily check-in calls and the two of them attended church together every Sunday, followed by lunch at the country club. The good news was that I could understand and empathize so completely since I could imagine one of my own daughters in the same circumstances . . . so I was particularly sensitive to Cathy's feeling.

CHAPTER 4

Howard and I married in North Carolina in February 1989, at the lodge at Hound Ears where my vacation cottage is located. We had planned our wedding at the little country church in Boone, but had to change venues at the last minute because of a driving but beautiful snowstorm. Because we wanted a small family wedding with only a few intimate friends, we couldn't possibly have married in Miami or Greenville as it would have taken on immense proportions.

Before moving to Greenville, I had been warned by family members as well as friends, to be prepared for the fact that small southern towns are often tightly inbred and not known for opening their arms to newcomers. Friendly, yes, and hospitable, but nonetheless closed. Often their children graduating from college, don't look for career opportunities nation-wide, but rather for the best job available in their home town .... Hence, there are many multi-generational families, and therefore inter-generational and intimate relationships among the townspeople.

Of course, I had the advantage of moving there with a long-time resident, whose first wife had been born and raised there and was a beloved daughter of the town. Still, it was an encouragement to me, the new bride, to have so many of her friends reach out to me ... There were parties of welcome, and soon I was invited to join one of the social dance clubs . . . I played bridge in her bridge club, and came to know her almost as if she had been a sister, particularly as I knew her children better.

We arrived in Greenville in late February and moved into Howard's townhouse to wait until our larger one was ready to be occupied. In early December, Cathy dropped by for a visit, and it was at this time that Howard mentioned that we would be going to Orlando for Christmas. Her reaction was an emotional storm, declaring passionately that she had never been separated from her father at Christmas, that she would always be a "daddy's girl" and this was not fair for him to be leaving at this special holiday, etc. and, sobbing pathetically, she ran out, slamming the door. I followed her, attempting to talk to her, but Howard insisted that I come back and let her calm down . . . I understood exactly her feelings as I had daughters of my own who might have had a similar reaction. I definitely wanted to follow her home and explain that we would make plans in the future to alternate special holidays between the two families... but since we were living there in the same town with her, it made sense to spend this first Christmas with my family in Florida. Just as I was preparing to go to her, the phone rang and it was Cathy, crying and pouring her heart out apologizing and begging me to forgive her and saying she loved me and didn't mean to be hurtful. I told her I thoroughly understood and thought it had been good to vent her feelings and that I hoped we always could be open with each other and could confront problems and talk them through. This proved to be a painful situation for the moment, which resulted in setting us on a warm and loving path for our future life together.

One idea that I believe was appreciated by both Howard's and my children: As we moved into our new condominium, we hung the family gallery in a prominent hallway. In the center was a picture of Howard and me at our wedding. On one side was a portrait of his late wife, along with special pictures from their children's youth. On the other side were my late husband and portraits of our three girls. In this way, they could come into our newly-formed family home and see that their loved ones had not been banished from our lives, but always would be remembered and honored.

Now to tell you about the venue in which I lived for the next 20 years of my life:

This I must say about Greenville, South Carolina, and I can say it objectively since I didn't grow up there, but came as an older adult:

Greenville is a small, sophisticated, southern city which offers incredibly broad opportunities . . . Located in the foothills of the Blue Ridge mountains, the climate is delightful, furnishing all seasons, with none of the severity of long hard icy winters . . . Spring is as beautiful as any place I've ever heard of, with dogwood trees blooming all over town, and the ground underneath blanketed in brightly colored azaleas . . . The Greenville Symphony is flourishing while so many others in much larger communities have failed; The Peace Center for the Performing Arts brings Broadway shows right out of New York; the County Art Museum features a fine permanent collection as well as excellent special showings, and the Sacred Art Collection at Bob Jones University is one of the finest and largest outside the Vatican, filling 16 expansive galleries . . . Greenville Little Theater brings outstanding live performances, giving opportunities for local professionals and amateurs to showcase their talent . . . Main Street is inviting, with small white lights strewn through the trees, and sidewalk cafes dotted from one end to the other . . . The city planners in recent years removed a downtown bridge, replacing it with a pedestrian one, exposing below the beautiful waterfall at Liberty Bridge Park . . . . The West End features a fine baseball stadium which houses the Minor League Greenville Drive, as well as art galleries and a plethora of tempting restaurants, from the elegant to the funky . . . All of this, plus the advantage of being home to Furman University where continuing education courses are available to the populace, make for a truly desirable environment. Greenville is located along Interstate 85, about halfway between Charlotte and Atlanta . . . Perhaps one of the reasons for the wealth and vitality of this small city is that it is the North American headquarters for several international companies, including Michelin, Hitachi and BMW.

Having said all that, I'm sure it's obvious that I fell in love with my new city. It was not a closed society, but welcomed this newcomer with open arms. We soon were blessed to become members of Mitchell Road Presbyterian Church where we worshiped and participated in all related activities, becoming part of the body life which was warm and loving.

I arrived in Greenville in February of 1989, and within the next year, had the opportunity to be the stand-in mother for Howard's children at both of their weddings in 1990 . . . In June, Paul married Leslie Loftus in Columbia where both were employed, and we had a wonderful time planning the rehearsal dinner and all the accompanying events. It was especially enjoyable for me, as he was my only son!

Then in November, Cathy married Sean Griffin. They had met while both were employed at the Greenville Chamber of Commerce . . . . It was such a delight for me, as I was well-practiced in weddings, having married off my own three daughters in recent years. All of my daughters and their families attended both Paul's and Cathy's weddings, and our two families began the blending process which has continued through the years so happily.

While in Greenville, we became involved in the political scene, drove for Meals On Wheels, enjoyed the art and music opportunities, and while Howard continued his activity with Executive Ministries Wednesday Morning Bible Study, I began teaching a weekly Bible Study in my neighborhood, as well as a monthly Circle

Study at church . . . We traveled to Israel, cruised to the Scandinavian countries, covered the Canadian Rockies, and spent several weeks touring England, Scotland, Ireland and Wales. Our lives were full and we were happy and fulfilled in our "second time around."

During these years, we were blessed with additional grandchildren, now totaling an even dozen, two of whom were Paul's twin boys, Hunter and Kyle, and one, Cathy's precious daughter Hartley. Besides Anne and Ed McDougall's Maggie and Jimmy, Claudia and Tom Waters' James and Cami, Emily and Terry Johnson contributed Drew, Sam, Sally, Abby and Ben. What a blessing to know that next generation!

In 2003, we began a time of trial and testing, as Howard was stricken with stomach cancer . . . He was in good physical condition as we both had given priority to working out and staying "in shape" through daily exercise . . . For that reason, he was able to undergo surgery to remove part of the stomach, and later part of a lung, only to return home to a normal, excellent quality of life. God had been so good as to provide us with a loving, caring group of friends, and particularly with a highly attentive and strengthening church body which enveloped us with love and encouragement.

In January of 2006, the cancer returned, this time to the spine . . . Once again the surgery allowed him to return home in comfort for a while, but we knew his time was limited . . . He was determined to live to attend granddaughter Maggie's wedding to young Jonathan Iverson, scheduled for June. We attended this special event in Orlando on June 24th, and a favorite picture is Howard and the bride on the dance floor.

. . . On September 29th, the Lord took him home and we mourned his going, while rejoicing in the knowledge that he was free of pain and in the presence of His Savior.

Part III

THE REST OF THE STORY
1895-2013

CHAPTER 1

As mentioned in the Introduction, there was a person who influenced my life more than any other, except for my parents . . . God used the Reverend Daniel Iverson "to guide me in the way of wisdom and lead me along straight paths." (Proverbs 4:11)

Young Dan Iverson's parents were missionaries to the dock people at the Seamen's Bethel in Savannah, Georgia. The family attended the beautiful historic Independent Presbyterian Church there, where Dan's father was an elder.

Annette Hartley

INDEPENDENT PRESBYTERIAN CHURCH

Founded 1755
As a Branch Of The Church Of Scotland

On a particular occasion, D. L Moody, the renowned preacher from Chicago, was holding a Bible Conference at the church. He had been a dinner guest of the Iversons at their home, where he had met young Dan. That evening he preached from the High Pulpit, from the Book of Daniel. He addressed the lad: "And young man, I want you to be a Daniel just like the one in the Bible some day." That occasion in 1895, was Dan Iverson's call to the ministry, and he did not waver from the call from that moment on.

In 1927 Preacher Dan Iverson was called to plant a church in the newly-incorporated city of Miami, Florida. His move there with his wife and five children, immediately followed the major hurricane of 1927. The storm had devastated the area., and his work began as a mercy ministry to those who had survived the natural disaster.

Twelve years later, in 1939, I attended his church plant, the Shenandoah Presbyterian Church, for the first time. I had attended Sunday School and Church with my parents all my life. We were a Christian family. Upon a special occasion, I spent Saturday night with a school friend and went to Sunday School at Shenandoah with her the next morning. I was 12 years old at the time, and it truly was a life-changing experience for me. I never had heard teaching like that. I learned that I actually could have a personal relationship with the God of the universe; that Jesus Christ loved me personally; and that I could know Him by giving my heart to Him and by reading His Word. "The Preacher" came to our junior high department and told us this himself.

At that time I believe God started me on His path. "Your Word is a lamp to my feet and a light for my path." (Psalm 119: 105)

I continued attending this church, where Mr. Iverson led me into a saving relationship with Christ. My parents soon joined me and we became members of this body of believers. Thereafter, The Preacher played an important role in my practical daily living. He not only preached to us, he led the high school bike hikes one Saturday a month, cooked our hot dogs, led our campfire singing, and every Sunday night after church, he led a "hymnsing" and testimony time for the youth.

Later on, he guided us through the years of World War II, holding regular prayer meetings for our boys in service, urging us to write them and let them know how much we appreciated their sacrifice.

His teaching and involvement in my life influenced my dating experience and my choice of a mate. I married a believer from another denomination, and offered to join his church with him, but he objected, proclaiming his admiration for Mr. Iverson, and he chose to join me at Shenandoah instead. The Preacher counseled us, officiated at our wedding, and baptized our first child, baby Anne.

Among my greatest blessings is the fact that my three daughters all are married to men of God who happen to be elders in the Presbyterian Church of America. I firmly believe that this direction was set in motion by the influence of "the Preacher" so many years ago.

Anne and her husband, Ed McDougall, live in Orlando, Florida and Ed is Director of the Florida Church Planting Network for the Presbyterian Church in America. Their daughter, Maggie, with her family, is on the mission field, and son Jim is active with his wife Rachel in a downtown PCA Church.

Claudia and her husband, Tom Waters, are deeply involved in a Presbyterian Church in Charlotte, North Carolina, where Tom serves as an elder. Their son James has gone on a number of short-term mission trips, and spent one year working with an inner-city mission in Newark, New Jersey under the leadership of Danny

Iverson III. On a regular basis, he handles lighting and sound at their church. Teen-age Cami, attends Covenant Day School in Charlotte, and works at her church, serving as volunteer at every opportunity. She also has been on two short-term mission trips, one to Honduras and one to inner-city Baltimore.

Emily and her husband, Terry Johnson, are in Savannah, Georgia where he is pastor of Independent Presbyterian Church. Their five children, ranging in age from 24 to 17 all are walking on God's path. Drew graduated from Wheaton College and is working in Savannah. Sam graduated from Wofford College and hopes to be accepted into Officers

Candidate School in the Marines this year. Sally is a graduate of the University of Georgia and will go on a month-long mission to Uganda before she starts her teaching at a Christian classical school. Abby is a student at Georgia where she is active in Reformed University Fellowship (RUF). Ben is a three-sport athlete at his high school.

What a blessing it is to see the next generations following on His path! And how grateful I am to God for leading me, at such a young age, to Shenandoah Church where I learned to love His Word and to know the joy of abiding in Him;

At Shenandoah, while only 21 years of age, I was asked to teach Bible in one of the Ladies' Circles. I was overwhelmed at the idea, for our church was filled with spiritually mature, godly women who had been teaching through the years. The three ladies who called on me with the suggestion, were former Sunday School teachers of mine. One of them offered to stay with baby Anne so I could attend, while the other two told me they would arrange to be placed in the Circle I was to teach, so they could be my support group, and there to help if I needed them.

As I reflect on that time, I can see that God used those dear ones whom I so revered, to start me on a lifetime of deep joy and satisfaction that comes from studying His Word in depth. What an honor to be given the opportunity to hold His tangible gift to us, His inerrant, infallible Word, which He breathed into existence, and to pass it on to others.

CHAPTER 2

2 7 years after "The Preacher" led me to Christ, and began to have such an influence on my life, I gave birth to my third daughter, Emily. At age 20, as related in Part I, Emily married the Reverend Terry L. Johnson, who had figured so helpfully during the time of grief over the seemingly untimely loss of her father. Terry was compassionate, wise and always accessible to us as we made our way through those very heartbreaking and difficult years. The wedding took place on May 23, 1986.

The following year, 1987, our young minister received a call from the historic and beautiful Independent Presbyterian Church of Savannah, Georgia. The church was founded in 1755 and was set apart by King George for the dissidents, many of whom were Scottish Presbyterians, who had settled in the area. Terry Johnson officially became the senior minister of this elegant downtown church, fully aware of the responsibility which was his. He was to help rebuild this once mighty fortress of the faith, which had gone the way of so many downtown churches, as the new wave of young families were moving out of town and to suburbia. His helpmate in this undertaking was 20-year old Emily, a willing and committed partner, but still a schoolgirl in tight jeans. My prayer, from the first day they arrived, was that God would grow the fruit of the Spirit in her life.

Although beset with the many problems which accompany the changes incurred when there is a ministry transfer, Terry was able to withstand the trials because he never doubted that God had called him to this place. After a time, those who were unhappy with the new minister left the church and the membership stabilized and began to build. Five healthy children were born to the minister's family, and this in itself led many young families to unite with the church, so that the nursery, which was practically empty and unused when they arrived, quickly grew to the point where multi-nurseries were required to serve the congregation.

Here I might inject that Emily's sadness and despair when Terry told her during their courtship that they could never be at home for Christmas because they had to be with their church family, of course became a moot subject as they provided their own warm and happy home in which to celebrate that beautiful season.

Now in 2013, Independent Presbyterian Church has continued to thrive and grow, is very much alive, having planted three other churches in the area, as well as seven more in various locations across the country, including one near the campus of the University of Georgia in Athens, one in California, others in Utah, New York, and Kansas.

And the Rev. Dr. Terry Johnson continues preaching from the very same high pulpit occupied by the renowned Dwight L. Moody when the young Dan Iverson was called to the ministry more than a hundred years before.

As I reflect on the seemingly untimely death of my dear husband of a heart attack at age 54, I now can see God's grace in the process. After the sad time of heartbreak and despair, He brought Terry into our home to help restore normalcy to our daily living. When I asked him whether he would have sought Emily as a wife had he not moved into our home, his honest reply was "No, she was just one of the girls in the Youth Group."

And so God's path led through sorrow and grief; but He spoke to my heart through those words from Isaiah

2:3: "Come let us go to the mountain of the Lord. He will teach us His ways so that we may walk in His paths." He took us through the agony and heartbreak and taught us His ways so that all of us would learn to walk on His path.

CHAPTER 3

Through the years, the only Iverson with whom
I stayed in touch was my contemporary, Bill, the
youngest son of Preacher Dan. The Reverend William
Thorpe Iverson and his lovely wife, Ann, had gone to Miami
Senior High School with Jimmy and me, and had visited
us in Miami from time to time with their three children.
Bill had been called to inner-city Newark, New Jersey, to
a cross-cultural ministry. Sadly, he lost Ann to cancer, and
later married one of her dear friends. Bill came to know
my second husband, Howard Hartley, and as might be
expected, given both of their warm and outgoing natures,
they formed an immediate bond. Bill had graduated from
Davidson and Howard from Duke, both colleges being
located in North Carolina, so there were a number of mutual
friends, discovered when Bill visited us in Greenville.

In June of 2005, Bill e-mailed me that he recently had
attended the weddings of two of his grandsons, both sons

of the Reverend Dan Iverson III, longtime missionary to Japan. I replied, "That's wonderful, but I'd always hoped there'd be an Iverson boy for granddaughter Maggie McDougall." Actually, I was just being facetious because that thought had not occurred to me before. Anyway, Bill e-mailed me back immediately, saying, "There's a great one left for Maggie; he's 26, a missionary with Mission to the World, and is on mission for a year in Sri Lanka to help rebuild after the tsunami."

Maggie had graduated from Davidson College in North Carolina, and was teaching school at the Norfolk Academy; and the Iverson grandson was Jonathan who had graduated from the University of Virginia before going to Morocco as a missionary. He had served there for two years before answering the call to help with the crisis in Sri Lanka which had been devastated by the tsunami.

Bill and I decided to introduce them by e-mail. We told both of them how our families had been interwoven through the years, sent them the respective e-mail addresses, and bowed out of the picture.

Jonathan began the correspondence July 4, 2005. Maggie found his letters witty and well-written and appealing to this English major, who, herself, had been gifted in writing. She also was impressed with his vocabulary and even had to look up some of the words; that didn't usually happen to her! She said, "Even if it didn't turn into anything, I just wanted to know him better and to be an encouragement to him while he lived overseas doing tsunami relief work."

In September, Jonathan had to make a trip to the States for his sister's wedding, which just happened to be in Virginia. He asked Maggie if he could come and meet her in Norfolk, to which she replied that she would love for him to come, but she didn't get off work until four, and Jonathan had to be in D.C. at Dulles by midnight for his return flight. Nonetheless, he drove down and they were able to spend several hours together. They took a walk through the historic section and shared an appetizer at a sidewalk café. I asked her if they had fun together and liked each other, and she replied with an enthusiastic affirmative. I, then, in grandmotherly mode, asked if he kissed her good-bye and she said, "Heavens no, Netsi, he just gave me a missionary hug". But her quote about Jonathan was, "I felt like we knew the same God", and after being with him that day, her earlier feelings were confirmed. "If there were men like Jonathan in the world, I didn't want to marry anyone else."

Upon his return to Sri Lanka, the correspondence became more engaged and intentional; there were phone calls, and Jonathan said he had planned to spend Christmas with his family in Japan, but under the circumstances, could he spend the holidays with her family in Orlando? Maggie learned later that this had been at the suggestion of her father and was thrilled at the idea. Anne and Ed of course knew of the long-distance romance that had been developing, and they were anxious to meet this young man.

Jonathan arrived at his grandparents' home in Waynesboro, Virginia, and picked Maggie up in Norfolk the next day. They drove to Orlando where they spent Christmas with the McDougalls, and Jonathan met and became acquainted with Anne and Ed and Maggie's brother, Jim. Maggie said it was a bit awkward at first, for her, but Jonathan kept it from being that way long by being so gracious and easy with everyone, and "we were able to process a lot of things in person without too many distractions, that we couldn't have done otherwise." For Anne and Ed, it truly was almost like an old-time family reunion since they had known other members of the Iverson family through the years. (Jonathan's great grandfather had baptized baby Anne in 1951!)

After a warm and delightful week in Orlando, Jonathan and Maggie went to Atlanta to spend New Years' with Jonathan's brother Joel and his wife, Mary Stuart. I happened to be in Atlanta at that time because my beloved University of Miami Hurricane football team was to play in the Peach Bowl at the Georgia Dome, and for Christmas I had given Terry and Emily and their five children tickets to the game.

Of course, Maggie and Jonathan had to come to our motel for breakfast so all of them could have the opportunity to meet Maggie's special friend. The children ranged in age from eight to seventeen and all were excited to meet this missionary they had heard so much about. Their father told them they were not to monopolize Jonathan, but that each one of them should think of one question they'd like to ask him. Naturally, they were all prepared when we got together, and eight-year old Benjamin got the last one: "What's the awful-est thing you ever had to eat over there?" Jonathan took all of this family involvement in stride, as he was one of nine himself!

My darling husband had not been well enough to make the trip to Atlanta, but he was deeply interested in Maggie and Jonathan's romance. He always had adored Maggie, and naturally wanted to meet this grandson of

Bill's who he had heard so much about. When they left Atlanta to return to Virginia, they drove up Highway 85, and Howard and I met them for lunch at the Chick-Fil-a, which was just outside the Greenville city limits. It was a happy and hilarious time with Howard coming on strong about "just what are your intentions where my granddaughter is concerned, young man?"

The young couple spent the last day and night at his grandparents' home in Waynesboro. The morning after they arrived, Jonathan and Maggie drove to an overlook on the nearby Blue Ridge Parkway, a favorite site of his, and where they had their first kiss two weeks earlier; it was here as they watched the sunrise, that he placed the ring on her finger. He shared with her then that he had asked her father as well as her brother for their permission to marry her. A blessed Christmas season for all concerned and what a joy to see how God had brought all this about!

The wedding took place the following June 24, 2006, at noon in the beautiful and historic Rollins College Chapel in Winter Park, Florida. The family ministers all participated, with the Rev. Terry Johnson officiating, and Jonathan's grandfather, the Rev. Bill Iverson, as well as his father, the Rev. Dan Iverson, presenting eulogies.

On the Friday night before the wedding, the rehearsal dinner was given by Jonathan's parents, Dan and Carol Iverson and their family, who had lived in Chiba, Japan for more than 20 years They entertained the large gathering with a Japanese feast, featuring lanterns and decor for the occasion.

Much attention was given to the most unusual means by which the bride and groom had met. In fact, in 21st century socializing, to have been introduced by their grandfather and grandmother, probably was truly unique. One of the ushers, before raising his toast to the bride and groom, announced at the microphone that he certainly was going to find more time to hang out with his grandparents.

Maggie and Jonathan, after honeymooning in the North Carolina mountains, settled in Orlando where Jonathan enrolled in Reformed Theological Seminary, to obtain a theological degree and become ordained as a minister in the Presbyterian Church of America. Maggie was given a teaching position at the Geneva School, where she continued working until their first baby, Anne Oliver Iverson, was born in December 2007. While there, another precious daughter, Lily Emeth, was born to them. Maggie said this period was "a hard but sweet time of community and safety and learning and adjusting."

CHAPTER 4

Howard's death, three months after the wedding, on September 29, 2006, was not tragic as Jim's had been. He was 82 and was in such terrible pain that death relieved him of the intense suffering, and there was a feeling almost of release to see him go peacefully, free from the agony of the dread cancer. However, the widow is still bereft, as well as lonely and needful . . . and still desiring to live a meaningful life for her remaining time on earth.

Having lived in Greenville for the last 18 years, and having it so filled with dear friends, a strong and supportive church, and feeling so cared for and loved by these people, the thought of moving away was unappealing in every way. However, I had no family living there, and although I was in good health, I knew that at my age, I had nowhere to go but down. Consequently, my thoughts turned to my three daughters, Claudia in Charlotte, Emily in Savannah and Anne in Orlando.

Savannah seemed the answer immediately because of the location: half way between Charlotte and Orlando. I waited for almost a year before I started to plan the move, as I needed that time to adjust to being without my beloved husband, and to bring myself to make such a momentous decision on my own. However, once more, I found that God walked with me through this. He was ever so near to me. He did not let me walk alone. He kept me on His path, the path He had chosen for me so many years ago.

As I prayed, pleading with Him not to let me make a mistake, asking Him to open and close doors to guide me in this whole new experience, I felt His constant leading. Something that I definitely was not giving thought to was a Retirement Community. I didn't want to move to an "old folks' home" although there was a lovely one on Skidaway Island in Savannah, which I had looked at briefly while checking out the possibilities in the vicinity.

Working with a knowledgeable realtor I had met at church, I located a beautiful condominium similar to the one Howard and I had in Greenville, and told the realtor I would be making financial arrangements for that when it became available in the next few months. However, I went home and simply could get no peace about it at all. Every night I prayed that God would show me it was right.

One night as I lay thinking about the whole questionable situation, I was given the strong feeling that I should go to The Marshes! It was a Retirement Community, the one on the island. I had looked at it but walked right out, knowing that I would not be moving into an "old folks' home!" Well, the Lord led me to reconsider. Without doubt He showed me that it would be right for me in every way! I went straight back to Savannah, made arrangements and moved in April 1, 2008. That's where I am today! I have found that the Lord truly led me to the "green pastures and still waters", the perfect place in which to spend my sunset years.

He still leads me on His path. I am privileged to worship each week at the same Independent Presbyterian Church in which the beloved evangelist Daniel Iverson was called to the ministry in 1895. God has allowed me the great privilege of teaching Bible in the monthly church circle, as well as in a weekly inter-denominational Bible study at The Marshes.

I do so want to "finish strong". I write and live with joy "being confident that He who began a good work in (me) will carry it on to completion until the day of Jesus Christ." (Philippians 1:6)

How blessed my life has been since that day when our Lord called me to Himself and started me "On His Path".

CPSIA information can be obtained at www.ICGtesting.com
Printed in the USA
LVOW06s0723310813

350251LV00001B/98/P